Freshwater Tackle

OUTDOOR LIFE TAKE-ALONG BOOKS

Freshwater Tackle

Baird Hall

Drawings by Tom Beecham

OUTDOOR LIFE • HARPER & ROW

NEW YORK • LONDON

CONTENTS

INTRODUCTION

For the past five summers, the author has been connected with a fishing school which, operating in three-day boarding sessions from May to September, has "graduated" more than 2,000 students. The men, women, and young folks attending these sessions ranked in experience from beginners to gray-headed old experts: young stockbrokers who didn't know one end of a fish pole from another and seasoned old sportsmen who were visiting the school between a stay at their Quebec fishing camp and a trip for salmon on Norway's Alta River.

A great truth became obvious in this contact with 2,000 fishermen. An expert with a salmon flyrod often doesn't know the basic elements of baitcasting for bass. Why should he? Or a thoroughly experienced spin fisherman may never have considered flyrodding for bluegills. And he *should* consider it, because it's wonderful sport.

The fisherman who wants to broaden his experience or a beginner out to wet his first line both share a common problem. A great deal has been written about every form of fishing, and there are many books that are well worth reading, but a man needs practical experience. In order to get that experience he needs the fundamental tools—fishing tackle.

This handbook is a concise presentation of the *basic* tackle required for spinning, baitcasting, and fly fishing. It is a simplified presentation of fundamental tackle and its use. It does not assume that the reader is an ignoramus, but that he wants to know the reason for selecting one piece of equipment against another. For any fisherman, expert or novice, has to find his way through a tremendous variety of available tackle. Simple, direct, and unprejudiced advice is not always easy to come by. And advice, unsupported by "reasons why," is not convincing and often not even clear.

The reader may already be familiar with some of the information presented in the following pages. My intent was not to be startling or original or abstruse, but to outline the well-established and proven fundamentals of tackle selection, and to back up these recommendations with commonsense reasons.

PART
I

Spinning
Tackle

1

THE MOST VERSATILE OF FISHING METHODS

Spinning tackle is now the most popular of all fishing methods. Many fishermen use nothing else and nearly *all* fishermen equip to spin on some occasions. To understand the principle of spinning, hold a large spool of thread between your thumb and finger, at top and bottom of the spool, and pull thread off so the spool turns. Now, grasp the spool between thumb and finger at its bottom end only, so the spool will not turn, and pull the thread past the free top. That's the way a spinning reel works. Fishing line pulls off the free end of a *stationary* spool; the reel's spool does not rotate.

This system has two practical advantages. Your line starts off the spool without the inertia-drag and friction caused by a turning spool, and when the line stops coming off, there is no inertia-spin of the spool to create a "backlash" (the overrun of a whirling spool that tangles the line).

The principle of drawing line off the end of a stationary spool is not new. But old-time fishing lines, when wet, didn't really peel off a stationary spool too well. Then along came synthetic monofilament lines which peeled off beautifully. Better spinning reels were devel-

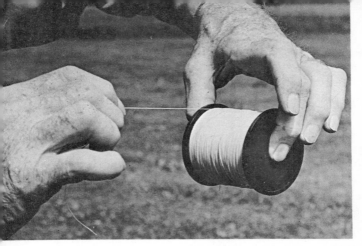

Spool of thread held as
shown in photo above
revolves as line is peeled
off, like a baitcasting
reel. Principle of spin-
ning reel is illustrated
in photo at right: the
spool does not revolve
and the line peels off
the end.

oped for winding the line back onto the stationary spool; monofilament lines were improved with respect to limpness, knot strength, and stretch. Spin fishing was really on its way.

The tremendous popularity of spinning is undoubtedly because it is the easiest way to toss out a bait or lure. A young child, in a few minutes, can learn to cast exciting distances—and with never a backlash. In fact, the ease of spinning understandably irritated many old-timers who had, over the years, perfected thumbing the revolving-spool baitcasting reel. And it tends to be resented by fly-fishing purists.

But of course there is a good deal more to successful fishing than the simple ability to hurl a bait at random a country mile. Later in this book we will be discussing baitcasting and fly-fishing tackle, and there is plenty to be said for the special advantages of these fishing methods.

The fact remains, however, that spinning *is* a wonderfully easy casting method. It *is* encouraging for beginners. It *is* very versatile, a method adaptable to taking just about every species of freshwater fish with just about every sort of lure in just about every sort of water. It is also true that spinning, however simple in its basics, can be refined to a high degree of sophistication. In short, spinning is simple for the beginner *and* can become a very subtle fishing method in the hands of an expert.

2

SPINNING REELS AND LINES

The Reel

Spinning reels divide into two classes, the open-face reel and the closed-face reel. The closed-face spinning reel, which includes all the so-called "pushbutton" models, is probably the most fool-proof casting instrument ever devised. Mounted on a rod so that the pushbutton is under the caster's thumb, pressure clamps the line during the rod's back and forward swing, release of thumb pressure lets the line go zipping out, a turn of the reel handle captures the line inside the reel case, and the caster simply cranks in his bait or lure. There is no chance of a back-lash because the spool under the nose cone is not rotating during the cast. If a fish takes on the retrieve, and it is too big or violent for the strength of the line, a preset slipping clutch lets the fish run a bit even if the excited fisherman keeps cranking furiously.

An open-face spinning reel requires a bit more manual work to operate. The caster hooks the line over his forefinger, swings back the bail, makes his cast and releases the line by straightening his forefinger. A turn of the reel handle snaps the bail to retrieve position. Again, there is no chance of a backlash because the spool

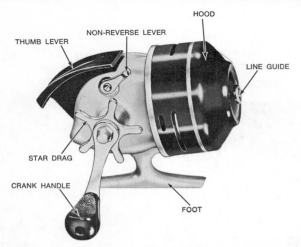

Closed-face spinning reel is mounted on top of the rod. Pressure on thumb lever (pushbutton) clamps line during rod's swing; releasing pressure frees line, which is carried off the reel by weight of lure.

Open-face spinning reel is mounted on underside of the rod. Operation of reel is shown in accompanying photos.

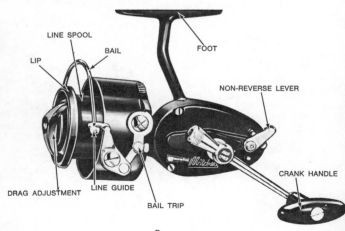

How to Cast with an
Open-Face Spinning Reel

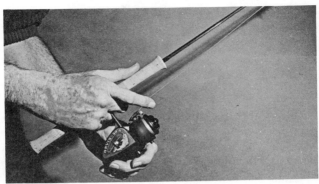

1. Holding rod with reel foot between second and third fingers, pick up line with index finger and release bail.

2. With line held in this position, bring rod back and forward...

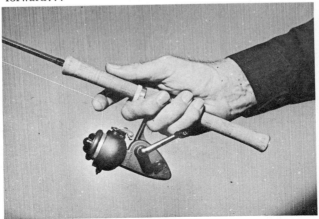

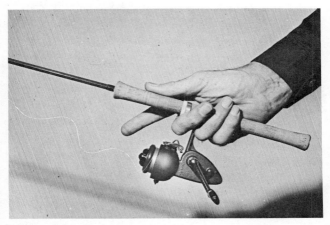

3. ...and extend index finger, releasing line and pointing rod tip at target.

4. Turning crank snaps bail into position, picking up line for the retrieve.

does not rotate during the cast. And again, a preset slipping clutch permits a fish to run if its pull exceeds the break-strength of the line.

Even though the open-face reel requires more manual dexterity, it is preferred over the closed-faced by many experienced and critical spin fishermen. A closed cone face slightly "feathers" the line as it spins off the fixed spool, and so reduces the length of a cast. The open-face reel permits a *deliberate* "feathering" of the uncoiling line with an educated forefinger, to drop the lure with pinpoint accuracy.

All open-face reels (but practically none of the closed face) cross-wind the line as it is retrieved. Cross-winding assures that the line will come off the spool more easily on the next cast, which again gives the open-face reel a distance advantage.

Generally speaking, the pushbutton type of closed-face reel makes a good trouble-free rig for the casual fisherman and for casting lures of more than ¼ ounce on lines of 6- to 10-pound test. The open-face reel is preferred for more critical spinning with ultralight lures from $\frac{1}{16}$ to ¼ ounce on 2- and 4-pound-test lines, and for heavier lures and lines when maximum-distance casts are important, maximum line control is desired, and the revolving roller on the bail is needed to reel in a big fish.

Just one word of caution. Whatever type of spinning reel you select, *invest in a good one* by a well-established manufacturer. In spinning, the reel is all important. It must be a precision instrument, well made, or it is absolutely worthless. Economize on rod, line, and lures if you choose, but even if you are just equipping young Junior for his first tries at sunfish, don't buy an unknown "bargain" spinning reel.

Setting the drag. As mentioned before, spinning reels are equipped with a slipping clutch —an adjustable "drag." The fisherman presets his drag below the break-strength of whatever test line he is using, so that the first yank of a viciously striking fish or a big fish's strong run won't snap the line.

Setting the drag is perfectly simple. The fisherman just has to remember two things. First, that the pull on his line may be a shock *yank* rather than a slow strain. Second, that the friction caused by the rod guides slightly increases line strain. In other words, he sets his drag *safely* below his line's break strength. Directions that come with your reel tell you how to increase or decrease drag pressure. Most closed-face reels adjust by rotating the nose cone or with a star wheel at the handle; most open-face reels by turning the nut on the spool's front face. In any case, experiment with your drag setting by mounting your line-loaded reel on your rod, locking the reel in retrieve position with its antireverse lever or by holding the handle, and yanking off line against the brake's resistance. Yank, don't simply pull. If you can possibly break the line, relax the drag setting until you can't. The setting obviously is more critical in ultralight spinning with 2- or 4-pound-test line than with 6-, 8-, or 10-pound test. A reel of good quality has a drag of good quality, a perfectly smooth, steady braking action. A shoddy "bargain" reel may have a drag that stutters and sticks.

Taking care of your reel. Maintenance of a spinning reel is not difficult. The good ones are made practically corrosion-free, so even dropping one in the water (*fresh* water) does no harm at all, unless mud or sand get into the works. Just keep your reel clean inside. Open up the front occasionally, swab it out, and put a couple of drops of light reel oil on all pivot points and moving parts. Then about once a season, open up the rear gear case, mop out all old grease (and dirt), and repack the gear case with light reel grease. It's worthwhile to provide yourself with a tube of special *reel* grease (many of which contain some graphite) because most ordinary greases are too heavy, stiffen in cold weather, and make your reel crank hard.

Just a word of caution. If you do happen to use your spinning reel in salt water, rinse it thoroughly with fresh water as soon as you get home, and relubricate it. The corrosive action and salt deposits of salt water are tough on equipment.

Spinning Lines

There are spinning lines of woven nylon or dacron and these have a few highly specialized uses. But for all practical purposes spinning line means *monofilament,* synthetic material extruded in a single, continuous strand and standardized in diameters rated for 2-pound test, 6, 8, on up to 20 pounds or more. The proper pound test (strength) for a man to fish with depends on what he is fishing for, and where.

In general, spin fishermen tend to buy and use line that is much too heavy. A 6-pound-test monofilament line of reliable well-known brand has immense strength. If you don't believe it, tie a 6-pound line to a powerful man swimmer and "play" him with a good, springy spin rod. You will be amazed.

There are two good reasons for a spin fisherman to use the *lightest* line practical for the fishing he expects to do. First, the lighter the line, the longer the cast. The lure's weight has to pull out the line, so the less it has to "carry" the farther it will go. And even the wind resistance on too large a line will noticeably reduce your casting distance. Secondly, the fatter your line is, the more visible it is to the fish. A bass, trout, panfish, any fish is affected by what's tied to your bait or lure. The lighter the line you use, the more strikes you will get.

Common sense tells you that if you have to "horse" an 8-pound largemouth out of wads of Florida grass you may need 10-pound-test monofilament to do it. But 2- or 4-pound-test monofilament can play a big crappie or bring a 4-pound brown trout to net in open water. And one thing is sure: you will end a season with more fish taken if you've used a line that occasionally breaks off than if you've used a line an angry shark couldn't pop.

Spin fishermen often argue that they need heavy monofilament to pull snagged lures out of logs. But if a man wants to fool a maximum number of fish, he will use line as light as can reasonably be expected to handle the *fish* he hopes to catch, not the logs. Six-pound-test monofilament is a good husky line for average fishing. Four-pound test is probably strong enough to handle most freshwater fish the average angler encounters, if he uses a limber spinning rod 6 feet in length or longer.

A reel spool should always be filled to within

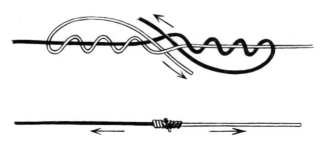

Barrel knot for joining two strands of monofilament.

about $\frac{1}{16}$ inch of its lip. If line comes up flush to the lip, it will spring off in coils. But if line is too far below the lip, it feeds out with resistance and shortens your casts. If break-offs shorten your line and you want to add line, first pull off enough so that the knot attaching the new line is well buried on the spool when the full length of a cast is out, so the knot won't cause your casts to jerk and stutter.

Loading a reel spool. To load your reel spool, mount the new-line spool on a pencil shaft so it will rotate, thread the line through the reel bail and crank the line on as though it were an ordinary retrieve.

A helper to hold the new-line spool on its pencil shaft is convenient, but it is perfectly possible to toggle up a rigging that permits the new-line spool to rotate without being hand-held. One way to keep a bit of tension on the line is to run it under a big book placed between the rotating new-line spool and the reel.

It is true (as you may have been warned) that every rotation of the reel bail puts one twist in the line. To rid your loaded reel of this twist, you can feed 200 feet or so of line down a running stream or out behind a moving boat and crank it in again. Actually, with lighter monofilament, the twists of original loading normally adjust themselves.

𝔅

SPINNING RODS

The grips on spinning rods divide into two general types: one for mounting the pushbutton type of closed-faced reel, the other for mounting open-faced reels. The rods designed for pushbutton reels (often called "spincast rods") are all made of glass. The rods designed for open-face reels are available in glass and also, for the critical spin fisherman, of six-segment bamboo.

Freshwater spinning rods are available in lengths from $5\frac{1}{2}$ to $7\frac{1}{2}$ feet, and in ultralight, light, medium, and heavy action. Rod length is mostly a matter of personal preference, but action should be determined by the weight of the lures you will be using. A short rod may have any action from ultralight to heavy and a 7-footer may also have any action from ultralight to heavy.

A true ultralight spinning rod is designed, in taper and action, to lay out tiny lures or live bait weighing from $\frac{1}{16}$ to $\frac{5}{16}$ of an ounce. A tiny spinner or a single worm on a 2- or 4-pound-test monofilament line is a combination for subtle and deadly fishing. And it is deadly for big fish—shy, wise, old 5-pound brown trout. The very limber slow action of a true ultralight rod protects the cobweb line from breakage and casts out soft-bodied live bait without snapping it off the hook.

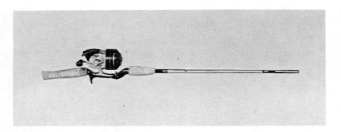

Rod for closed-face spinning reel, often called a spincast rod, mounts reel on top, has grip for index finger.

Light- and medium-action spinning rods are designed for lure weights from ¼ to ½ ounce, and for line tests of from 4 to 8 pounds.

Perhaps it is fair to say that most spin fishermen, just as they use lines too heavy, also tend to use rods too stiff for the fishing they do. It's a lot more fun to play a fish on a lively, limber rod than on a stick that feels stiff and "clubby."

Spinning rod for open-face reel has straight grip.

And a ¼-ounce lure casts much better on a rod it can *flex*. It should be the spring of the rod that does the work, not the exertions of the caster.

So if a man intends to do most of his fishing with ¼-ounce lures, he would do well to select a spinning rod that flexes *clear down to the butt* while casting lures of that weight. The rods with medium action and heavy-duty action are for lures of ½ or ⅝ ounce, which will flex *them* down to the butt.

Fly-and-Spin rod has a sliding reel seat to mount spinning reel at mid-grip or fly reel at butt.

There is a special group of spinning rods, available in glass or bamboo, called "Fly-and-Spin." These are basically flyrods designed with a level cork grip which mounts a fly reel at the butt end or, interchangeably, an open-face spinning reel at mid-grip. A flyrod rigged for spinning is a very efficient casting tool. These rods come in sizes from a tiny 5-foot fairy wand (casts 5-weight flyline and spinning lures of $\frac{1}{16}$ to $\frac{1}{8}$ ounce) to a 8½-foot heavy-duty model (casts 9-weight flyline and big spinning lures for steelhead). The general-purpose model is a 6½-foot rod taking a 6-weight flyline. With a spinning reel, it will cast ¼-ounce lures a country mile with pinpoint accuracy.

Any spinning rod that has a good "feel" to *you* and that flexes well with the casting weight you plan to use is probably worth exactly the price asked for it—this in distinction to a cheap spinning reel which may be worth less than nothing.

Most spinning rods are made of glass. More expensive rods, of bamboo, are used mostly by specialists for ultralight spinning. The subtle, extra responsiveness of bamboo is most noticeable, of course, when casting tiny lures or live bait on cobweb-thin monofilament line.

Bamboo rods have metal ferrules joining their two or more sections together. The better the bamboo rod, the tighter the ferrules fit. Some glass rods are made with glass self-ferrules, but a glass rod of fine quality may also have very close-fitting ferrules. The least bit of oxidation or film of soil can cause ferrules to stick—sometimes so tightly that one man cannot pull them apart. Don't ever grip sticking ferrules with pliers or any other tool. And when you get a friend to help you pull, don't put him on one end of the rod and yourself on the other. Both of you should grasp both sections, exactly as though each were doing the job alone. This method requires an odd crisscrossing of arms, but it will pull stuck ferrules apart without breaking the rod.

Once the rod is apart, resist the temptation angrily to sand down the male ferrule. Just clean it with alcohol or soap and water, and swab out the female ferrule. Ferrules should be clean, dry, and tight-fitting. Greasing a ferrule alongside your nose is bad practice. Grease simply adds to the film of soil that makes ferrules stick.

4

FISHING WITH SPINNING TACKLE

Live and Natural Baits

When fishing live or natural bait—worms or live minnows, "laced" dead minnows or frogs—the smart fisherman uses little or no weight. A sinker damps the action of bait and dulls the feel of a taking fish.

Suppose you want to cast a single, lightly hooked, wildly wiggling angleworm to a beaver-pond brook trout, or even a *piece* of worm on a tiny hook to a pond bluegill. An open-face spinning reel loaded with 2- or 4-pound-test monofilament and a limber rod will cast that single worm respectable distances with no sinker, not even a split shot. It is one of the most effective approaches.

If you hook a lively little minnow through the lips or carefully high on the back in front of the dorsal fin, you want him to swim *almost* free. You do not want a sinker. With a spinning reel, you can cast this bait way out without any abrupt *snap* to tear it off the hook.

Because you can lob out your bait without any shock, you can hook a worm very lightly and just *once* through its "collar." Very often the natural look of such light hooking can make all the difference in fooling a wary fish. Your worm can drift and move freely, instead of being looped like a pretzel and wadded into an inert mass.

A single salmon egg can be set delicately on the very point of your hook. This is not always necessary. Several eggs in a little nylon net (made from a piece of your wife's discarded nylon stocking) may be effective and is certainly very sturdy on your hook. But single-egg fishing is often the way to get the most takes, and the smooth gentle motion of a lobbing spin cast is the way to toss a single egg way out there.

Of course, if you want your live, struggling minnow down near the bottom of the pond, or you want to bump your worm along the bottom of a swift stream, you may have to add a bit of weight—one or two split shot pinched onto your line, or, if the stream is really fast, even a sinker. But a good bait fisherman always uses the *least* weight he can get away with.

If you do have to use a sinker, put it on the *end* of your line, with your bait on a dropper line, so that when a fish takes there is no lead between it and the reel. This way, you can lower your rod tip to give slack to a nibbler, thus pre-

When fishing live bait, attach sinker to *end* of line, with bait attached to a dropper line. To make a dropper line, use the barrel knot (Chapter 2), leaving one end long.

Bubble attached to end of line provides weight for casting fly on dropper line.

venting the cautious fish from feeling resistance and dropping the bait. And when you do strike to set the hook, you are striking the *fish,* not a hunk of lead.

This principle also applies when you are using a spinning bubble. The various spinning bubbles available are an excellent way to add casting weight when you need it. An empty bubble floats and will give you casting weight to toss out anything from a dry fly to a natural grasshopper. You can also fill the bubble with water and it will sink your bait for more subtle bottom bumping and less snagging than you get with a lead sinker.

Poppers and Bugs

More exciting than live bait are surface lures, the floating plugs and poppers which are widely useful but perhaps have a special appeal for bass. The fisherman who concentrates on big trophy bass tends to use baitcasting tackle, as discussed in the next section, but for bass up to 4 pounds, and particularly for casting surface lures, spinning tackle is very efficient.

Surface spinning lures (*from top*): ¼-ounce Hula Popper which pops and bubbles when twitched; ¼-ounce Sputterbug whose propeller makes a trail of bubbles; ¼-ounce Jitterbug with a clumsy swimming motion.

The scoop-faced floaters that pop and burble when twitched, the propeller surface runners that churn a path of bubbles on retrieve, the surface wobblers that swim with frantic clumsiness—all are successful. Color is probably less important in surface lures than in deep-running plugs because, viewed from the dark depths against a light sky, the color of a surface lure doesn't show much. But bass are very unpredictable, and all bass men accumulate lures of many colors and many actions.

There is no thrill in all sport fishing to match the shock of an old mossback exploding from under a surface lure. It's always a shock, no matter how attentively a man is watching his lure.

The only problem with spinning tackle for surface lures is, so to speak, a problem in reverse. Casting is so easy with spinning tackle that a man can get careless and lazy and not practice for much accuracy. When lures go sailing way out with a mere flick of the wrist, it's a temptation to be satisfied with rather sloppy casts. But surface poppers should often be delivered with pinpoint accuracy, close to or even *onto* a lily pad, into narrow channels among dead flooded trees, or right up against a grassy bank.

Accuracy is really easy enough with spinning tackle. Practice makes perfect. A good idea is always to cast for a particular spot, always, even when you're working the middle of a pond and it makes no real difference just where your lure lands. Nonetheless, always pick a particular spot and ding your lure as close to it as you can. Make a habit of this and before you know it you'll be an accurate caster. It can pay off big on occasion, especially in the close quarters common to work with surface lures.

The Colorful Plugs

Underwater lures are more various than the top-water class, and even the spin fisherman who is sticking just to *basics* must equip himself a bit more generously: three classes (plugs, spoons, spinners); three levels (shallow runners, middle runners, deep runners); more colors.

Plugs by the hundred are offered to fishermen, each one advertised as a "killer," and many of them actually are. But the wise fisherman makes sure, before buying on simple impulse, that he is equipped for *all three levels*—a plug or two that retrieves shallow, one or two for retrieving at middle depth, and one or two deep-running plugs. It's no use to "fish where they ain't." A man must be able to experiment for the depth at which fish are on a particular day at a particular place. If his plug runs at the wrong level he may get no strikes no matter what its miracle action and no matter what its color.

Not that color can't be important on occasion. All the Sunfish family (which includes the basses as well as bluegills and crappies) can be fussy. The pikes as well as the basses are excited by yellow. Red-and-white bright plugs can be good one day; on another day, dull plugs and "naturals" with scale finish get strikes. As much *variety* as a man can afford is all to the good.

In fact *variety*, not only in colors but in actions, is the thing to strive for in selecting even a most limited collection of lures. Don't begin with four plugs by different makers that fundamentally behave the same way. A propeller lure runs straight and splashy, a floating lip-lure makes little plunges on erratic retrieve, another lip-lure is designed to plunge deep, a jointed lure is designed to writhe and wriggle. Build a lure collection, right from the start, for variety in actions and colors.

The single most valuable thing to remember is that fish go for a *live thing in distress*. A

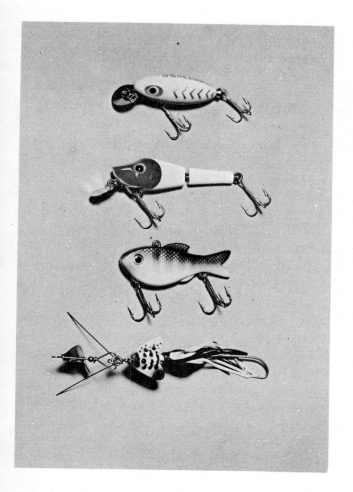

Spinning plugs (*from top*): ¼-ounce Hula Dancer, a floater which dives on retrieve; ¼-ounce Rib Lip, a slow-sinking swimmer for medium depths; ¼-ounce Tru Shad, a sinker for more depth; Hawaiian Wiggler with weed guard, for bottom bumping.

terrestrial (land-based) creature that falls into the water or an injured minnow—these are the easy prey—and predatory fish know this well. The sight and the sound of a cripple in the water is the surest thing to fetch a strike. All plugs, whether surface or shallow runners or deep runners, can be fished with an action which suggests a live creature injured or distressed (or occasionally rushing frantically to escape capture). Take the time, with each plug you buy, to swish it back and forth on a short line in clear water, to study its particular action at various speeds, at steady motion, at stop and go. Dramatize that plug as a living creature in distress, and you will take more fish with it.

Spoons, Spinners, and Jigs

The wobbler spoons and the rotating spinners, like the plugs, are selected for variety according to the depth they run. All spoons and spinners naturally sink, but their differences in design as well as weight determine the level at which they retrieve when cranked in at the speed which develops their proper action. Sounds complicated. Well, it is, a little.

In simple terms, the heavy, narrow spoons and spinners are the bottom bumpers and are designed for a relatively fast retrieve. The lighter, wider spoons and spinners develop their proper action at a slower retrieve and can be run at shallower depths.

There are many highly painted and bedizened spoons and spinners. Fundamentally, the variety necessary is gold, silver, copper, red-and-white for spoons, and gold, silver, copper, and black for spinners. Fancy painting and feathered trims are perhaps mostly an effort to identify a particular manufacturer's version of a basic shape.

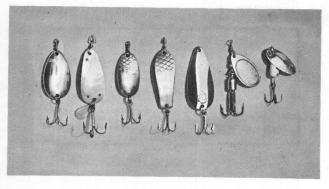

Spoons and spinners (*from left*): Swiss Broad Spoon; Pear Wobbler; Medium Spoon; Narrow Spoon; Red-and-White Dardevle; Mepps Spinner; Panther Martin Spinner.

Decoration doesn't hinder but probably doesn't help much. Plain gold, silver, copper, and the traditional red-and-white stripe are a good start in spoons. They should be of sound design from a well-known maker and in various weights from $\frac{1}{16}$ to $\frac{5}{8}$ ounce. Plain gold, silver, copper, and dull black are enough color variety in spinners, plus variety in weights and actions.

Heavy-headed jigs for bottom bumping ride with the hook *up*, reducing the chances of snagging.

Jigs are in a class by themselves. They were designed and originally used for saltwater fishing. But in the smaller sizes they have proved deadly on occasion in fresh water, particularly for bottom-fishing lakes and ponds.

Jigs are fished by letting them sink to the bottom, then bouncing or jigging them with the rod tip. Because of the design of the weighted head, a jig rides hook up, which reduces snagging to a minimum. You can start the jigging motion on the bottom, but also you can retrieve a foot or two at intervals and often locate fish at different levels.

One caution: Having originally been designed for saltwater use, jigs tend to be available on big hooks, and these hooks tend to be coarse. For freshwater work, buy the smallest jigs you can find, and, using your hook hone, keep the jig's hook *needle sharp*.

Ultralight Spinning

Fly fishermen, particularly the trout flyrodders, tend to regard spinning as a sport for infants and idiots. Well, ultralight spinning is highly sophisticated, and as a method for taking a suspicious lunker brown trout in a low, clear stream of late summer (the ultimate test), it is probably the last word.

"Ultralight" does not mean fishing with one of those stubby, stiff little sticks generally labeled as ultralight. It means casting tiny spoons and spinners of $\frac{1}{32}$, $\frac{1}{16}$, or at most $\frac{1}{8}$ ounce, using

Selection of $\frac{1}{8}$-ounce lures for ultralight spinning.

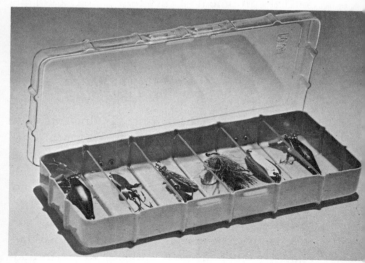

monofilament line of 2- or 4-pound test, and a rod which, regardless of its actual weight, is long enough and *limber* enough to be flexed its full length by those tiny, light lures.

Fly fishermen often speak of "fishing fine and far off." Four-pound test monofilament is as *fine* as a 5X tippet. The proper rod will toss a ⅛-ounce lure a country mile, definitely *far off*. The spinning line always sinks, while the fly fisherman's leader often floats, and on very still ponds or pools of low, clear water, the sunken fine spinning line is much less obvious than any floating flyline.

So ultralight spinning is a very subtle approach to shy fish in today's hard-fished waters. It is a rather specialized sport and requires specialized equipment: a very limber rod, an open-faced reel with a sensitive, smooth drag, 2- or 4-pound-test line. But it will take big trout when no other method will.

Spinning Tips

"Pumping" a fish. Setting the drag on your spin reel (as discussed in Chapter 2) means adjusting the drag *safely* below the break point of your line. Sometimes you may find yourself hooked to a fish so large or so strong that your "safe" drag setting will not crank him in. In this case, you "pump" your fish—that is, you raise your rod slowly up to vertical without cranking, then drop it quickly to horizontal, rapidly cranking in the slack. This pumping action will bring your fish to net when simple cranking would merely slip the drag and not retrieve line at all.

Line twist. Much is said about using a swivel just ahead of a lure to avoid line twist. Well, it is doubtful that even the most free-turning swivel can in fact accomplish this purpose. Constant twisting of monofilament line will cause the line suddenly and distressingly to spring off the reel spool in a wild tangle. Your best course is to avoid the use of any lure with overall rotation. A spinner should spin on its own shaft, without rotating the shaft which is attached to your line.

However, the best of spinners and even many wobbling spoons, if retrieved faster than their designer intended, can put some twist in line. So it is a healthy idea, every now and then through a day's fishing, to detach your lure and feed your line down a stream's current or out behind a moving boat. A free line in the water will quickly relieve itself of twist, so let it run out beyond the length of your longest casts, then simply crank it back in, reattach your lure, and proceed merrily with your fishing.

Steady trolling especially requires watchfullness for line twist, but spinning tackle makes an almost ideal rig for freshwater trolling. Your safe drag setting means that a striking fish gets hooked, but its first run (contrary to your boat's direction) is taken care of by the slipping drag. It gives you time to get things under control. Of course, the appropriate spinning rod for trolling must be stiffer than for ultralight spinning, and your line test heavier than 4 pounds. Spinning tackle, however, is thoroughly efficient for trolling.

Baitcasting Tackle

5

THE BIG-FISH TACKLE

"Baitcasting" has come to be the generic term for all fishing with a revolving-spool casting reel. A baitcasting rig can be used with plugs, spoons, and spinners. It can also be used for trolling. This reel is often referred to as "level wind" because nearly all models nowadays have a mechanism to cross-wind line as it is retrieved so it will pay out smoothly on the next cast. Until monofilament made spinning practical, the revolving-spool reel was everyman's casting reel. Now it has become almost the specialist's tool—the specialist in big fish.

There are many expert casters who feel that, if a man will take the time and trouble to learn to handle a revolving-spool reel really well, it provides a degree of accuracy and control un-equalled by spin equipment. This may be merely because most spin fishermen, as admitted in Part I, are satisfied with long casts and are inclined not to practice for absolute accuracy. It would appear that a practised expert at ultra-light spinning *can* develop great accuracy, plus enjoying spinning's undeniable advantage at lay-ing out ⅛ ounce lures. But for handling heavy lures with lines testing stronger than 10 pounds, the revolving-spool reel is still supreme. As evidence of this, manufacturers not only continue making baitcasting reels but are continuously improving them with free-spool designs, new antibacklash devices, new closer tolerances to permit the use of monofilament lines.

𝕮

THE NEW BAITCASTING REELS

The most obvious difficulty in learning to cast with a revolving-spool reel is in learning to control the backlash. With a lure sailing out on a vigorous cast, the reel spool spins faster and faster as line peels off. A whirling spool, by the law of inertia, tends to keep on spinning. So, as the lure begins to slow in flight and finally comes to full stop in the water, the spool tends to keep on peeling off line and can create a wildly tangled mess.

With an "educated thumb" the fisherman can apply light braking pressure on the whirling spool and can learn to control this over-running. Now manufacturers are advertising a "thumbs-off, no backlash" device. This is an oil film brake with automatic variable pressure. It is available, of course, only on the more expensive models. It may not always fully control backlash without a watchful thumb. It may create a little resistance which would shorten the cast unless heavy lures are used. But it is a wonderful improvement for casting big lures on 15-pound-test monofilament.

The second difficulty with baitcasting reels again involves the law of inertia—this time as it applies to the energy required to start the spool spinning. And since most baitcasting reels have a geared-in level-wind device, the starting resistance could considerably cut down the distance of a cast. To counteract this, revolving-spool casting reels are available with a "free-spool" device. This disconnects the level-wind mechanism to let the spool run free on the outward cast.

FREE-SPOOL LEVER

LEVEL-WIND MECHANISM

STAR DRAG

Revolving-spool baitcasting reel with level-wind mechanism, star drag, and free-spool device.

Baitcasting reels are available with a "star-drag" mechanism which, like the slipping clutch on a spinning reel, can be set below the break-strength of your line and permits a heavy fish to run without the fisherman's releasing the reel crank.

Revolving-spool casting reels are being steadily improved, and not the least of the improvements is a much closer tolerance between spool and rims. If your line jumps the spool and jams between spool and rim you are in serious trouble with a fish on and in for considerable exasperation. Even braided lines can do this, and monofilament lines have a special genius for getting themselves so caught. Monofilament is now very popular for baitcasting reels. All in all, a man is probably wise to invest enough money in his reel to assure the close tolerance.

In fact, since the baitcasting reel has become primarily a specialist's tool for handling big fish, a good model by a reputable manufacturer is probably sound sense. The casual now-and-then fisherman has turned almost entirely to spinning. The baitcaster is a specialist who expects to put in some real practice to perfect his technique. In this connection, expert baitcasters who have perfected "thumbing" their reels can argue that a revolving spool reel actually "shoots" line and so, properly handled, can give as much distance as a spinning reel which spins off line in coils to be "feathered" by a guide.

7

BAITCASTING RODS

Traditionally, baitcasting rods have been shorter and stiffer than the other types—4 to 6 feet as compared to 6 to 7 feet for spinning rods and 7 to 9 feet for flyrods. Baitcasting rods tend to have a "steeper" taper—that is, a very stiff butt tapered to an "action" tip. This tendency can be overdone: a butt that feels like a club and a tip too weak to set a big hook in a striking fish. A baitcasting rod, like *any* rod, really should flex its full length when casting the maximum weight lure for which it was designed.

This problem becomes more acute for the bass fisherman than for the steelheader. A man tossing a ⅝-ounce lure into a rushing torrent for steelhead needs a powerful rod, powerful from butt to tip. But the bass baitcaster, using 10-pound line to lead a largemouth out of weed tangles, may wish to use lures of ¼ ounce or less. So for the bass man, accuracy and casting ease require a rod that can develop action with ¼-ounce lures, and this action should not be entirely in the tip. A wobbly tip distorts the cast and may fail to sink the hook barb when you strike the taking fish.

In substance, then, a man selecting a baitcasting rod will wisely do two things. First, he will

Baitcasting rod has offset handle for mounting reel on top.

face squarely the range of lure weights he pro-
poses to use with his rod: light action for lures
of ¼ ounce and less, medium action for lures of
½ ounce, medium-heavy action for lures above
⅝ ounce. One rod will *not* work satisfactorily
for all weights. Secondly, our man will attach
the selected weight to a rod tip and wave it,
even if he has to do this right in the store. He
will wave the rod back and forth, watching to
see that the given weight *does* produce at least
slight flex in the butt while not giving the tip
an excessive bow.

Rod with bad flex (*left*)
has a stiff butt and
weak, floppy tip. Rod
with proper flex (*right*)
has a smooth curve from
butt to tip.

Good action is not always a matter of price. Of course, fine rodmakers label their rods with great care for the weights they are designed to cast. But a "bargain" baitcasting rod may really be a bargain—poor guides, a tip-top that wears, winds that come loose and ferrules that don't keep their fit—and still be a rod of satisfactory "action" and perhaps worth the money asked.

A baitcasting rod can, of course, be used for stillfishing from bank or boat, and it makes an excellent freshwater trolling rod (in fact, the rods specifically named "trolling rods" are for saltwater work). But in selecting a baitcasting rod, you should consider its ability to *cast* the lures you will be using, then stillfish or troll with it as secondary considerations. The only exceptions to this rule are the special cases touched on in the next chapter.

FISHING WITH BAITCASTING TACKLE

Baitcasting Lines

As mentioned earlier, a revolving-spool reel is not only supreme in its friction-free ability to crank in a heavy fish but is also best able to handle the heavier lines required to hold big fish. Monofilament line above 10-pound test does not spool well on a freshwater spinning reel. And a great many baitcasters still prefer to use *braided* line anyway, which does not behave well at all on a spinning reel.

With a revolving-spool reel, a man has complete freedom of choice between braided line or monofilament line *and* the ability to troll deep for salmon and lake trout with wire trolling line or lead-core trolling line.

Soft-braided dacron and nylon lines are readily available in strengths from 10-pound test up. These are supple, will not rot or mildew. They are not "invisible" so the fisherman ties on 2 or 3 feet of monofilament leader between line tip and the lure or bait.

Monofilament line is its own "leader," even in 10-pound-test size. It is as true in baitcasting as in spinning that "the lighter the line, the longer the cast." Of course, a heavy lure can carry out quite a weight of line, but it is still important to use line no heavier than you really *need*. Ten-pound test is, in fact, strong enough for big bass even in weeds and grass, and your lures for bass aren't very heavy. Big, heavy lures for muskies or steelhead might move your line up in weight, almost as much because of the shock-stress of casting the lure as for fighting the fish.

Of course, if a man owns a rig used exclusively for trolling big lures for big fish, he can ignore all considerations of casting distances and go in for as much heft as makes him feel secure in his mind. This is particularly true of deep trolling for lake trout, for instance, with wire or lead-core trolling line. In fact, lead-core line starts at 15-pound test or more.

Baits and Lures

The more frail and delicate live baits are best cast with a very limber spinning rod, because this provides the least shock on the cast (which could snap off frail bait) and maximum distance.

But again, the bass man is the major problem here. He may need 10-pound line and a revolving-spool reel and relatively light bait. Fortunately, a hellgrammite attaches on a hook fairly securely. A small frog can be secured in a frog harness. With a baitcasting rig, a man can learn to lob live bait gently and accurately for fair distances, and he can cast or troll a securely laced baitfish.

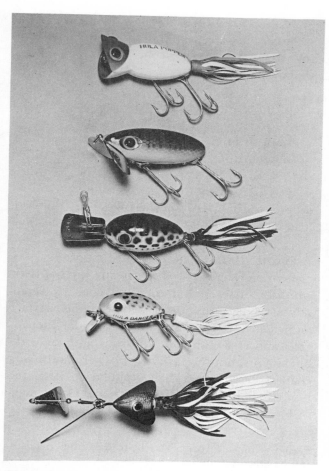

Baitcasting lures (*from top*): ½-ounce Hula Popper, a
surface floater that pops when twitched; ½-ounce Jitterbug, a surface splashing swimmer; ½-ounce Arbo-Gaster,
a floating plug that dives on retrieve; ½-ounce Hula
Dancer, a sinking plug for medium depth; ½-ounce Hawaiian Wiggler, bumps along bottom without snagging.

The *artificial* lures for bass, as for other fish of larger size, are available in ½-ounce baitcasting weights as well as in ¼-ounce spinning weights. The surface poppers and runners, the underwater shallow runners, the underwater deep runners are all much the same as were discussed in Chapter 4.

Again, it might be stressed that a man is wise to choose his lures for variety of action at different levels (surface, shallow, deep) before going in heavily for variations in colors and the minor differences in appearance as offered by different lure makers.

Plastic worms. There is one important newcomer on the list of artificial lures—plastic worms. These are almost in a class by themselves. They can be fished on the surface (crawled over lily pads), and just under the surface, and cast with spinning rods with or without sinkers, but they are listed in this baitcasting chapter because of their popularity with the big-bass baitcasters. Often they are fished deep in big impoundments like the TVA lakes.

Plastic worm, a favorite with baitcasters after big bass, can be fished on the surface or deep.

Plastic worms are available in natural brown, black, purple and many other colors, with purple, of all unlikely shades, being especially deadly.

Deep trolling for lakers is a rather specialized sport. The fish may be down 60 feet or more, which means wire or lead-core line to get down there and a flashing succession of spinners to attract fish in these gloomy depths. But trolling with a combination of spinners and bait or lure is widely practiced for all sorts of fish at more reasonable depths.

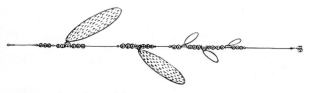

Flashing spinners for deep-trolling with lead-core line.

Trolling, with a laced minnow or with a good lure, does have a tendency to twist the line. It may help to put a swivel into your terminal rigging, but don't depend too much on it. Every half hour or so of steady trolling, unsnap your lure and let your line run free behind the boat for a minute or two to relieve itself of twist. Line twist is nowhere near as serious a menace for the baitcaster as for the spin fisherman. With a spinning reel, a twisted line is very likely to

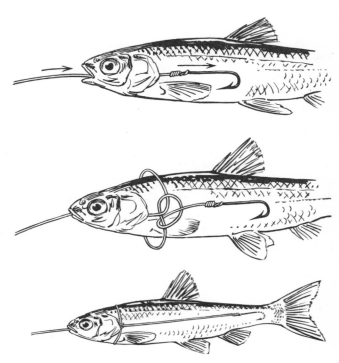

Method of lacing a minnow for trolling.

leap off the stationary spool like a live thing—in a wild tangle which is virtually impossible to straighten out. With a revolving spool reel, a twisted line simply develops little kinks which can warn a watchful fisherman that his lure must be rotating. He can unsnap his lure, relieve the twist as described above, and if he is wise, substitute a lure which does not rotate when retrieved or trolled at the speed he wishes to use.

Actually, a baitcasting outfit is the preferred rig for trolling. And, as previously stated, also preferable for heavy line fishing. As a casting outfit it requires much more practice than spinning, but the men who do take the trouble to perfect their technique swear by it—especially for big bass.

Fly
Fishing
Tackle

THE APPEAL OF FLY FISHING

The flyrod rates at the top in the sport of fishing. All fishermen know this and many bitterly resent its being so stated, the resentment arising from several misunderstandings.

There exist the notions that fly fishing is very difficult, requires a special skill, and is practiced only by a few idle, rich snobs anyway. Well, learning to lay out a flyline is no more difficult than learning to spincast, and is much *less* difficult than learning to cope with a revolving-spool reel. The awesome "mystique" which attaches to fly fishing is simply because a man *can* develop his skill and knowledge endlessly, and many men have dedicated whole lifetimes to doing just that.

In other words, anybody can become a fly fisherman in half an hour. It requires no more time or money or special skill than any other fishing. But because of the special fascinations and scope of the sport, many fly fishermen do become fanatical about it. They study to become experts in entomology (bug life) and stream ecology. They study the finest subtleties of rod actions and line balances. The rich ones spend large sums of money practicing the sport. The literary ones write books about it. And

altogether these zealots tend to give fly fishing a
very bad name with the ordinary guy.

Many, many "ordinary guys" do fly fish, however, for it truly does offer special thrills. Virtually all experienced fishermen, all sportswriters for instance, name the flyrod as their
greatest love. It is the most interesting way to
present surface bugs, poppers, streamer flies to
bass. It enables panfish, even the small ones, to
fight with the spirit of true gamefish. It is traditionally the preferred way to take trout and
salmon.

The central fact about fly fishing is that you
cast the weight of the line instead of the weight
of the lure—that is, a heavy flyline carries forward a featherlight lure instead of a heavy lure's
pulling out a light line as in baitcasting and spinning. Not all flyrod lures are in fact feathers, but
they are all almost weightless. And it is the *lines*
which are given weight numbers (in grains),
whereas spinning or baitcasting *lures* are given
weight numbers (in ounces).

So flyrods are designed each to cast a particular weight of line. We might start with these
mechanics and then work back to just why flyrodding is considered to be the best sport in all
fishing.

10

FLYRODS AND REELS

If a man is going to own one flyrod and do a lot of different kinds of fishing with it, he wants an 8-foot rod designed for an 8-weight flyline. This one rod can lay out big wind-resistant bass bugs and streamer flies and also small dry flies. An 8-footer for 8-weight line is the all-purpose rod which can fish a big Alaskan river and a small New England trout stream and Florida's bassy backwaters.

However, if a man knows that most of his fishing is going to be on big water for big fish with big lures, he may choose an 8½-foot rod designed for a 9-weight flyline. This bigger rod is still fine for big bass bugs, and still not too heavy for all-day one-handed casting on a steelhead or salmon river.

On the other hand, if a man wants a rod exclusively for trout and panfish he should consider a 7½- or 8-foot rod designed for a 6-weight flyline, or perhaps even a very delicate 7½-footer designed for a 5-weight line. One of the enormous advantages of fly fishing is *delicacy of presentation* in today's hardfished waters. When a man specializes on trout and panfish, or can afford an extra rod just for this extra delicacy, it will pay off in more strikes. In fact, the fashion in flyrods has undergone a great change in recent years. Not long ago, 12-foot rods were common and a 9-foot rod was considered rather short. Nowadays an 8-footer for 8-weight flyline is "all purpose" and a 7½-footer for 6-weight flyline is actually the most popular. And many fly fishermen are equipping themselves with delicate wands of 7, 6, even 5 feet, for line weights of 6, 5, and 4.

This is because, as stated above, delicate presentation pays off in more strikes. The man who is fishing for trout and panfish today is not usually fishing wilderness waters where the fish have never seen a human being. Today's fish don't grab at anything presented any old way. So ultralight flyrods are not a stunt. They serve a special purpose for today's difficult fishing and will be discussed later, in Chapter 12.

Another rod specialty is the so-called "pack rod." This is a mechanical rather than a fishing distinction. Most modern flyrods are 2-piece. A 6½- or 7-foot pack rod takes down to 3 or 4 pieces, so it will pack only 26 or 24 inches long.

The makers of fine flyrods, both in glass and the more sensitive bamboo, mark their rods plainly as to the line weight recommended to bring out the action of each rod. A line too light simply does not flex a rod, a line too heavy overloads a rod, and either difficulty makes it hard or even impossible to lay out long, smooth casts. Line improperly matched to the rod is largely responsible for the notion that flycasting is difficult to learn. With proper matching of rod and line, the cast turns over and straightens out with perfect ease. As stated earlier, anybody can be taught to flycast in half an hour.

Are bamboo flyrods really better than glass? Well, a fine bamboo flyrod costs five times the price of glass, yet very knowledgeable fishermen buy them (by no means always the rich fishermen either). Yes, there is a "feel," responsiveness, and liveliness to bamboo not matched in glass. But the difference is subtle. It is really apparent in the more delicate (light line) weights. If a man's major sporting interest is fishing and he does a great deal of it, he will probably ultimately invest in bamboo. But good glass flyrods are very good indeed nowadays.

It is at least true that a good glass rod is better than a rod of cheap bamboo. Bamboo must be selected and worked (by hand) by rodmakers of great skill and judgment. Glass rods are manufactured on a mass-production basis.

Whether of bamboo or glass, it is largely the *taper* of a flyrod's design that distinguishes the good from the mediocre from the bad. Within limits a good rod may be stiffish (fast action) or very limber (slow action) as a matter of the fisherman's personal preference. Fast action feels crisp, and the timing of your cast is more critical. Slow action feels easy and relaxed and your timing can be less precise.

But a rod long or short, fast action or slow or medium, must flex its full length, from tip clear down into the butt, when casting the line weight for which it was designed. As with spinning rods,

Strobe-flash photo of a flyrod during the forward cast shows, in position second from right, the smooth curve from rod tip down to grip which is the mark of proper flex.

a clubby, stiff butt and weak, floppy tip would distort the cast. A rod with full-length flex is fairly easy to identify, even in a crowded store. And make sure that you know the recommended matching line weight for the rod you buy.

The Fly Reel

Choice of a reel is the least critical part of assembling a fly-fishing outfit. A single-action (one turn per one wind) reel by any reputable maker is perfectly adequate. Multiplying reels (one turn per 2 or 2½ winds) are available for more rapid line recovery, something of a comfort when you are fishing all day on a big river. And automatic reels are available which spring-wind in the line at the touch of a lever. An automatic has limited capacity, so it is not good if a man wants "backing" line behind his 30-yard flyline.

"Backing" line is normally 20-pound-test braided dacron, spliced behind the flyline, in case a heavy fish makes a long run. It is not needed, of course, for small fish, but if you want 50, 100, or even 150 yards of backing, you must buy a fly reel big enough for your flyline plus the backing. That is, your fly reel may be rated for "WF8F line or WF7F line plus 100 yds. backing." Twenty-pound-test braided dacron backing line is available in spools from 100 to 1,000 yards.

To mount backing behind your flyline is a bit of a chore, made easier if you have a line

Single-action fly reel: one turn of the handle winds on one turn of the line.

Multiplying fly reel: one turn of the handle winds on two turns of the line.

Automatic fly reel: fingertip touch of lever activates spring and winds on line.

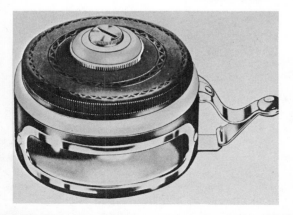

changer but perfectly possible with a spare old reel. First mount your new line on your new reel. Loosely knot backing line to the flyline, then wind backing on *over* the flyline until the reel spool is filled to within ⅛ inch of its rim. Now unwind the backing onto a line changer or onto an old spare reel. Then unwind the flyline into large loops on a clean carpet or around the back of a handy chair. Then transfer the backing line from the line changer or old spare reel onto the new fly reel. Fasten the back end of the flyline to the backing line with a nail knot, wind the flyline onto the new reel *over* the backing, and the job is done.

Incidentally, many fly fishermen purchase an extra spool for their fly reel so they can carry one floating line and one sinking line for the same reel.

11

FLYLINES AND LEADERS

The Line

All flyline used to be made of silk and identified by letters for diameter size. Size A, for instance, was a diameter measure and, being always silk, also indicated a certain weight. Then along came nylon, and permanent floating lines, and the old diameter measures became misleading. Size A lines might be of different weights depending on who made the line out of what material. But it is a certain weight a man wants to work his rod properly. So flylines have now been given numbers based on the actual weight of the first 30 feet of the line.

FLYLINE WEIGHT TABLE

(based on the front 30 feet of line)

No. 1	60 grains		No. 7	185 grains
No. 2	80 grains		No. 8	210 grains
No. 3	100 grains		No. 9	240 grains
No. 4	120 grains		No. 10	280 grains
No. 5	140 grains		No. 11	330 grains
No. 6	160 grains		No. 12	380 grains

A flyrod designed to cast a 6-weight line, for example, is designed to be flexed best by 160 grains of weight.

Besides differing in weights, flylines also differ in "shape." A "level" (L) line is the same diameter its full length. A "double-taper" (DT) line starts small, tapers to a larger diameter, then back to the small diameter. A "weight-forward taper" (WF) starts small, tapers up to bigger diameter then back to a small diameter more quickly than the "double taper."

Some flylines are so made that their specific gravity is less than water; they float. Some are made so their specific gravity is greater than water; they sink.

A flyline is plainly marked. For example, a line marked WF6F is weight forward (WF), 160 grains (6), and it floats (F). One marked DT6S is double taper, 160 grains, and sinks (S).

About the only virtue of a level flyline is that it costs much less than a weight-forward or double-taper line. It is the most difficult to cast, and presents a fly with less delicacy. A double-taper line is much easier to cast, and delivers a fly with less splash. But actually a weight-forward line is easiest of all to cast and, with its lighter running line closer behind the fatter belly, it "shoots" through the guides more easily, giving you extra distance when you want it. So a man buying an all-purpose 8-foot for 8-weight rod does well to buy a WF8F line. Or, if his rod is the 7½-foot for 6-weight trouter, a WF6F line. The front taper of a WF (weight forward) line may be just as gradual (and so as delicate) as a

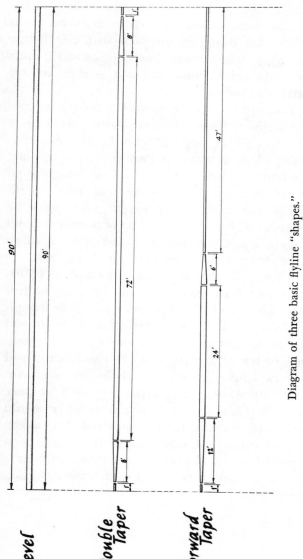

Diagram of three basic flyline "shapes."

DT (double taper). And for most of his fishing, wet flies and nymphs as well as dries, he wants a line that floats. So the man with one flyline wants a *weight-forward, floating* line and it must have the weight number listed as right for his particular rod.

There are, however, special occasions for special flylines. Take an early-season day with a stream running high and murky and no trout rising. A man wants to bump a nymph along the bottom where the big trout are lying doggo, so he uses a sinking flyline that will get his nymph down, even in a current. Or suppose he wants to inch his fly along the bottom of a pond —again a sinking line, cast and allowed to go clear down before retrieving in little jerks.

There are also the new "sink-tip" (ST) flylines that float except for the forward 10 feet or so which sink. This carries a wet fly or nymph well down under, yet leaves most of the line on the surface where you can watch it for the telltale twitch of a taking fish. It also enables you to·pick up the line more easily for the next cast.

Whether a line is an F (floater), an S (sinker), or an ST (sink-tip), the *weight number* should always be the same for the same rod. And again, if you carry just one flyline, it should be a *weight-forward floater.* Your leader will let a wet fly or nymph go under even with a floating line.

Leaders

The monofilament tied between the front end of a flyline and the fly is one of the most vital parts of a fly-fishing rig. This leader costs only pennies, yet it can make a caster's life miserable or make every cast a joy, depending on whether the leader is right or wrong.

A leader should not be made of the limp monofilament used for spinning line. The butt end, attached to the flyline, must be big enough and stiff enough to carry the line's thrust on forward along the unfurling leader. The leader must taper down to its "point," which must be small enough to let the fly float naturally on or in the water. The longer the leader and the finer its tippet point, the more strikes a man gets.

Standard compound tapered leaders are available in 7½-, 9-, and 12-foot lengths. A properly tapered leader of good material will turn over (and lie straight) almost as easily whether it's 12 or 7 feet long. Just how long a leader should be, and how fine its tippet depend on two factors: the size of the fly and the type of water.

A leader's tippet diameter must be matched to the size of fly to be cast. A very fine tippet will collapse with a very large fly. A tippet too big will not let a small fly swim naturally.

In rough, fast water you can use a shorter leader and a bigger tippet point. Smooth, still water demands more leader and a finer tippet.

Leader monofilament is available in kit with instructions for tying leaders; contains 14 spools of different diameters, from .021″ butt size down to .004″ tippet size.

TIPPET SIZE TABLE

Tippet Size	Fly Size	Tippet Size	Fly Size
0X	2 to 1/0	4X	12, 14, 16
1X	4, 6, 8	5X	14, 16, 18
2X	6, 8, 10	6X	16, 18, 20, 22
3X	10, 12, 14	7X	18, 20, 22, 28

Obviously, the fisherman who is laying out a big size 4 bass bug, and must move a striking bass quickly away from the lily pads, must use a 1X tippet (which tests about 9 pounds). But the man who wants plenty of strikes from sunfish in a still pond or who hopes to fool a wary brown trout in low, clear water, must go down to at least a 4X tippet (which tests a bit less than 4 pounds).

If, instead of buying ready-made compound-tapered leaders, you wish to tie your own, you can get spools of leader material (which is *not* limp spinning line). Using the barrel knot, you can graduate the various lengths in the various strengths as shown:

SPECIFICATIONS: 7½ FT. TAPERED TROUT LEADERS

0X	1X	2X
24″–.019″	24″–.019″	24″–.019″
16″–.017″	16″–.017″	16″–.017″
14″–.015″	14″–.015″	14″–.015″
9″–.013″	9″–.013″	9″–.013″
9″–.012″	9″–.011″	9″–.011″
18″–.011″	18″–.010″	18″–.009″

3X	4X
24″–.019″	24″–.019″
16″–.017″	16″–.017″
14″–.015″	14″–.015″
6″–.013″	6″–.013″
6″–.011″	6″–.011″
6″–.009″	6″–.009″
18″–.008″	18″–.007″

9 ft. Tapered Trout Leaders

0X	1X	2X
36″—.021″	36″—.021″	36″—.021″
16″—.019″	16″—.019″	16″—.019″
12″—.017″	12″—.017″	12″—.017″
8″—.015″	8″—.015″	8″—.015″
8″—.013″	8″—.013″	8″—.013″
8″—.012″	8″—.012″	8″—.011″
20″—.011″	20″—.010″	20″—.009″

3X	4X	5X
36″—.021″	36″—.021″	28″—.021
16″—.019″	16″—.019″	14″—.019
12″—.017″	12″—.017″	12″—.017
6″—.015″	6″—.015″	10″—.015
6″—.013″	6″—.013″	6″—.013
6″—.011″	6″—.011″	6″—.011
6″—.009″	6″—.009″	6″—.009
20″—.008″	20″—.007″	6″—.007
		20″—.006

12 ft. Tapered Trout Leaders

4X	5X	6X
36″—.021″	36″—.021″	36″—.021″
24″—.019″	24″—.019″	24″—.019″
16″—.017″	16″—.017″	16″—.017″
12″—.015″	12″—.015″	12″—.015″
7″—.013″	7″—.013″	7″—.013″
7″—.011″	7″—.011″	7″—.011″
7″—.009″	7″—.009″	7″—.009″
7″—.008″	7″—.008″	7″—.007″
28″—.007″	28″—.006″	28″—.005″

7½ FT. SALMON, STEELHEAD, BASS BUG LEADERS

Extra Light .021—.011	Light .021—.013	Medium .021—.015
18″—.021	26″—.021	26″—.021
16″—.019	22″—.019	23″—.019
14″—.017	12″—.017	21″—.017
12″—.015	10″—.015	20″—.015
10″—.013	20″—.013	
20″—.011		

Heavy .021—.017	Extra Heavy .023—.019
36″—.021	36″—.023
34″—.019	34″—.021
20″—.017	20″—.019

Even if you do buy ready-made leaders, you'll want to carry little flat spools of tippet material at least in sizes 4X and 5X. Fine leader tips do break off. Also, changing flies gradually reduces the length of your fine point. You want to be able to tie on a fresh tippet point occasionally.

Leader material, being a stiffer monofilament than limp spinning line, has a "memory." That is, when stored in small coils it tends to stay in coils instead of lying out straight when you cast it. A leader lying on the water in coils is not good. Fortunately, this is easy to correct. Simply carry a little piece of old innertube in your fishing-vest pocket. Pinch the leader between two of the folded rubber surfaces and pull it through. One or two pulls through will straighten the leader.

Attaching leader to flyline. At least one manufacturer now makes flylines with a monofilament front-end loop. A short length of large-diameter monofilament is epoxy-spliced into the flyline's front end. This front-end loop and the loop of your leader butt are instantly and easily joined.

Flyline with monofilament loop for attaching leader.

It is a great convenience because you may well want to change your leader on the stream, to switch from a 12-foot 5X dry-fly leader to a 7½-foot 3X leader to put a streamer through a fast riffle, or to replace a broken leader with a new one of the same size.

If your flyline does not have a front-end loop, snip off the leader's butt-end loop and fasten the leader butt to the line tip with either a nail knot or a needle knot.

If the above knots seem a bit complicated for streamside leader changing, particularly in the dusk and excitement of an evening rise, you can always fall back on that fisherman's friend, the tucked sheet bend.

This is simple to tie and amply secure. It is not quite as free-running through guides and tip-top as the very smooth nail or needle knots, but it is one of the neatest and least bulky of easily tied knots.

Nail Knot

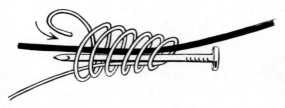

1. Hold a smooth nail along the line and wrap leader six or more turns around nail and line.

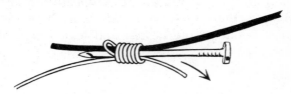

2. Thread end of leader along nail, under the turns.

3. Withdraw the nail and, holding the turns between thumb and finger, pull line and leader until knot is snug.

4. Trim ends of leader and line and fray end of line that protrudes so it will pass frcely through rod guides.

Needle Knot

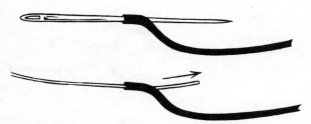

1. Use a needle with an eye large enough to take 20-pound-test hard monofilament (.025″). Stick the point through the center of the line tip, then out through the side. Allow the needle to remain in place for a while, then remove it.

2. Push the end of the leader through hole formed by the needle and out the side. Lay the needle along the line, wrap the leader around needle and line (as in the nail knot), then run end of leader through the eye.

3. Pull the end of the leader through the turns, carefully, so they stay in place.

4. Finally, tighten the knot and trim off end of leader.

Tucked Sheet Bend

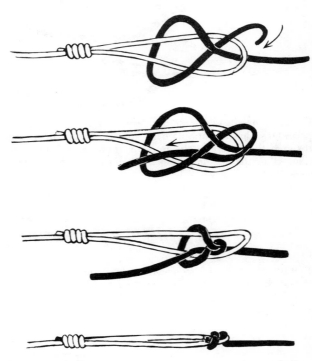

This is an easily tied knot for joining leader to flyline.
The flyline is threaded through the loop of the leader, as
shown, and the knot pulled tight and the end trimmed.

12

FISHING WITH FLY TACKLE

There are still a few fishermen who use a flyrod to fish bait—worms or minnows or salmon eggs or such. The long, limber rod, the thick flyline that doesn't tangle easily, have some virtue for poking through a hole in the brush to dap bait. The rig for this rather special purpose is a short (2-foot) monofilament leader on the end of the flyline, with a split shot 6 inches above the hook to steer the bait straight down into the water.

For casting live bait, however, spin rigs have definitely taken over. And in point of fact, ultra-light spin rigs are also best for all the little spoons, spinners, and plugs frequently labeled "flyrod size."

The flyrod is a tool exclusively for laying out the artificial bugs, spiders, flies, and streamers that are virtually weightless. It is a tool to turn over a heavy line to carry out the wonderfully subtle and deceptive lures that can be cast only this way and that are especially exciting to fish with.

Bass and Panfish

One of the best rigs for bass fishing is an 8-foot flyrod for 8-weight line, a 9-foot leader tapered from .021 to a .01 inch point (1X), and a dozen assorted lures. For surface fishing, these may include a hair frog, a tiny dish-faced popper with breathing maribou trim and wiggly rubber legs, and a big hairwing Gray Wulff dry fly. For underwater work, a Muddler Minnow and a bright Mickey Finn streamer are usually productive.

A little practice in bass territory and a fisherman discovers that by "false casting"—keeping his line in the air, back-and-front, back-and-front, back-and-front—he can zero in on his target with perfect accuracy. He can drop his lure beside an old stump or onto a particular lily

Selection of flyrod lures for bass: hair bugs, balsa poppers, big dry flies and streamers.

pad. His practically weightless lure is subtly deceptive. And when the unsuspecting old bronzeback busts it and the whippy rod plays his every move, a man gets the special exhilaration that makes flyrodding for bass practically an incurable disease.

On the other hand, a man who equips light for panfish has many hours of great sport readily at hand. With a 7½-foot rod for 6-weight line, a 9- or 12-foot leader tapered to a 5X point, and some tiny rubber-legged spiders and wet and dry flies, he can have as much fun with a bluegill as with the larger gamefish.

Trout

Since early times, fishing with flies has been the most popular method of angling for trout. The beginner may be perplexed by the various types of flies in use today, so it's probably a good idea to explain how they differ and how they are fished.

Dry flies are tied to float on the surface of the water. These flies are usually designed to imitate aquatic insects which have risen to the surface to hatch and fly away.

Wet flies are tied to imitate dead aquatic insects that have fallen into the stream and are being washed along by the current.

Nymphs are tied to imitate the underwater stage of aquatic insects, before they hatch on the surface.

Selection of flies for trout (*top row*): 2 dries, 2 nymphs; (*middle*) terrestrials; (*bottom*) streamers.

Streamers imitate small baitfish upon which bigger fish feed.

Terrestrials are flies which imitate land-based insects that have fallen into the stream—ants, grasshoppers, beetles.

When a specific hatch is in progress, trout feed greedily and conspicuously. The real hatching flies have to float long enough to dry their wings, and trout come to the surface and gobble them. The fisherman lucky enough to be present at this time tries to "match the hatch" with an artificial, from his fly box, which is about the

size and color of the natural. Aquatic insects
hatch (emerge) in the same rotation every year.
The study of this (entomology) can occupy a
lifetime and still leave plenty a man doesn't
know.

As a crude starter: The first hatches of April
tend to be gray (Quill Gordon, for example).
The hatches from May to June tend to be brown
(March Brown). The hatches from June through
July tend to be cream (Light Cahill). A man
tries to see what's hatching and match it, for
color and size. When in doubt he probably uses
a mixed gray-brown Adams and he may do very
well with it. Dry-fly sizes for trout may range
from big 10s and 12s down to tiny midges size
20. The fisherman observes what is "coming off"
the water and tries to match it for size.

Since a dry fly is supposed to float, fly tyers
make an earnest effort to use very light hooks
and buoyant materials. But flies of different pat-
terns vary considerably in natural floatability,
and no fly will continue to float if it gets soaked
through or covered with slime from a fish's
mouthing. So a dry fly has to be "dressed" with
a liquid, a spray, or plain grease. Modern dry-
fly liquids or sprays are silicone in suspension
in isopropyl alcohol. Isopropyl alcohol mixes instantly with water so if you dip or spray a fly
and toss it out still wet it will sink like a stone.
But isopropyl alcohol evaporates *very* rapidly,
so if you dip or spray your fly and blow it dry
it leaves every fibre nicely coated with silicone.

If a fish has mouthed a fly, you must wash it thoroughly in the stream and blow it dry, then spray or dip it in dressing and blow it dry again before resuming casting. Mucilin, line dressing, or even Vaseline make very durable floatants, but they mat the hackles and, once a treated fly does start to sink, it has to be steam-cleaned before it can be retreated.

Dry-fly fishing to visibly rising (feeding) fish is exciting and the easiest form of the sport; however, 90 percent of a trout's diet is underwater food, and very largely the nymphal form of the aquatic insects. Fortunately, a trout feeding underwater is not likely to be quite as selective as during a hatch. So, a generally buggy wet fly or nymph, drifted to his underwater feeding station, may well get a strike. Zug Bug, March Brown Nymph, Breadcrust, and Picket Pin are such generally buggy silhouettes, suggestive of many of the aquatic insect forms found in trout streams. For most wet-fly and nymph fishing a floating line is fine. The leader lets the wet fly sink enough to be visible to the fish in fairly shallow or slow water. In the high, fast waters of early season or in some lakes, where it is necessary to get the nymph right down on the bottom, you may need a special sinking (or sink-tip) flyline, as previously discussed.

From midsummer to the end of the trout season, after the major mayfly hatches are over, the so-called "terrestrials" are effective flies—the ant, grasshopper, or beetle. It is here in low, clear midsummer water that long leaders (12 feet or more) and fine tippet points (4X, 5X, even 6X) are almost essential.

Streamer flies, the imitations of baitfish (Muddler Minnow and Mickey Finn are examples), are most easily fished in fast water and riffles. The fish in such locations have less time to study a food offering, so heavier and shorter leaders can be used without reducing your strikes. Fish, in pursuit of what they believe to be a live minnow, strike hard, and fast water can give them a big advantage, so this is not the place to use fine leader tippets.

Advantages of Fly Fishing

The special fascination of fly fishing perhaps has to be experienced before it can be fully understood. There is a rhythm and a beauty to laying out a flyline that is deeply satisfying. But there are also definite practical advantages to flyrodding that can be explained in words.

In surface fishing for bass, for instance, the tiny poppers, bugs, and dry flies for the flyrod are the most subtle and deceptive. There are times and places where this subtlety may not be necessary, where pugnacious bass will smack any lure. But it never hurts to use a lure that can actually fool a wary fish, for even the most pugnacious bass is not actually determined to commit suicide. In heavily fished waters, the more stupid bass get caught when they are small. But even to a smart old bass a fluttering Gray Wulff looks like a moth in distress.

The specialist in lunker bass, the man who hunts fewer fish but the biggest, does most of his fishing down deep. But the man whose pleasure is the heart-stopping explosion of a surfacing bass gets most strikes on flyrod lures. Incidentally, the biggest bass hit tiny lures when they will surface at all.

As mentioned before, false casting a flyline enables a man to set down his lure with absolute precision, on the spot he means to hit. This is true even when that spot is down a long, narrow aisle between a mass of old stumps. Bass have a way of hiding out in spots like that.

Panfishing with a flyrod is a whole new world of sport—new, that is, to the man who thinks panfish are for kids. Many sportswriters have voted fly fishing for bluegills as seriously rivaling fly fishing for trout. And whether it's bluegills or trout, this is the place to put in a pitch for the ultralight flyrods, a special class of sticks with a special charm of their own.

Ultralight Flyrods

These rods were given passing mention in Chapter 10, rods tapered for flylines of 6 weight, 5 weight, 4 weight. Such rods range in length from 7½ feet down to tiny "banties" only 5 feet long and weighing 1½ ounces.

What these flyrods have in common is a casting feel like a fairy wand, and the ability to let a bluegill or 2-pound rainbow fight like a tiger.

Good fishermen can and do subdue 30-pound
Atlantic salmon with a 6-foot rod weighing 1⅞
ounces. But the real purpose of the ultralights
is to lay out small flies with exquisite delicacy
to the kind of average-size wary fish found in
the hardfished waters of today.

A 7-foot, 2-ounce ultralight glass flyrod designed for a
5-weight line—the Golden Eagle by Orvis of Vermont.

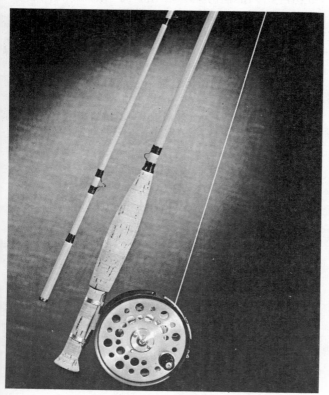

A 7½-foot rod for 6-weight line is a delightful and practical tool, no specialist's tool at all. And at least one manufacturer offers, in both glass and bamboo, a rod called the Midge which is a 7½-footer for 5-weight flyline. The Midge rod got its name as a rod for laying out the tiny #20 and #28 midge dry flies, but it will put out big #10s and #12s perfectly well. It is of course a very limber rod of slow action. Slow action, as mentioned earlier in this book, gives easy, relaxed casting and requires much less critical timing than the snap of a fast-action rod. It is easier to learn to cast with a slow-action rod, and it is certainly beautiful to watch the easy, effortless motion of man and rod and unfurling line.

Any notion that fishing with exaggeratedly light tackle is especially "sporting" or "elegant" is ridiculous. But tackle light enough to fool a fish into striking and to feel a fish during its battle makes very good sense indeed.

The ultralight flyrods let you feel every move of your fish. Their steady, limber pressure can subdue fish up to 6 or 8 pounds easily, but these rods will flex to lay out long casts of light flyline. Light flylines and long leaders tapered to fine tippet points get more strikes (many more) from sophisticated, wary fish in relatively quiet waters.

If a man fishes mostly small or quiet water, for trout or panfish, he will do well to consider a 7½-foot rod for 6-weight line or even an ultralight 7½-footer for 5-weight line. And if a man does need an 8-footer for 8-weight to pry bass out of heavy weeds, he would do well to start saving his nickles for a second rod. Because in the low, clear water of a midsummer trout stream, or the much-fished water of everybody's favorite bluegill pond, the ultralight outfit will take fish when nothing else will.

And as for fun and excitement, the ultralights are sort of the essence of flyrodding. When fish are finicky, when spinning and baitcasting lures look coarse and heavy, when even a #8 flyline stands out like a hauser and a size 12 fly sits on the water like sweeping from a dustpan . . . that's when you sail out a light #5 flyline, unfurl a 12-foot leader with a 5X tippet, and a tiny 16 or 20 Black Ant. A 16-inch brownie lying hidden alongside a treefall in a bare 2½-feet of water swings out and sucks in the Ant. And what happens then in that shallow water is what makes fly fishermen such stubborn nuts. There is no fishing quite the equal of fly fishing.

PART
IV

General
Fishing
Equipment

13

ACCESSORIES

Waders and Hip Boots

Many fishermen, and particularly fly fishermen, get into position for casting by wading. The best equipment for this is a pair of chest-high waders, waterproof almost to the armpits. These are made with attached bootfeet, or with soft stocking feet worn with wading shoes. The boot-foot waders or the wading shoes should have *felt soles* for sure footing on slippery, rocky stream bottoms.

Also available are hip-high wading boots, less expensive and more comfortable than full-length waders. Both waders and hip-highs are available with rubber soles instead of felt, at less cost. If a man does much wading, however, he does well to grit his teeth and invest in full-length waders with felt soles. The much more secure footing, and the ability to go deep, keep a man's attention on his fishing instead of his wading. He will take more fish.

Fishing Vest

Many fishermen, but again especially fly fishermen, need a fishing vest. This garment is not simply an article of clothing but is designed for

Fly fisherman's vest with diagram of storage pockets.

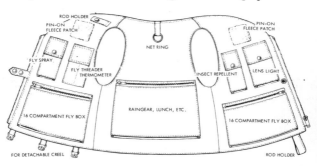

Outside

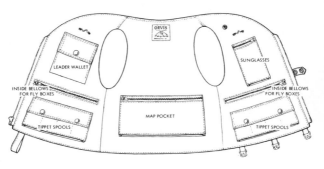

Inside

convenient storage of the equipment a man needs readily when he's wading.

A proper vest should stow dry-fly spray to clean and float flies, clippers to snip monofilament, tippet spools to replace shortening leader points, a collection of fly and/or lure boxes.

Accessories for the fly fisherman (*bottom row*): hook hone and angler's clippers; (*top row*), illuminated magnifier for tying on flies at dusk; tippet spools; dry-fly spray.

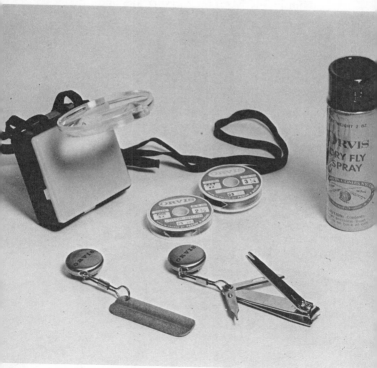

Fly-and-Lure Boxes

A good collection of flat, inexpensive plastic fly-and-lure boxes is a convenience even for the man who does his fishing from a boat and can carry along a big tacklebox. The flat boxes become a "filing system" to keep flies and lures properly sorted and free of tangles.

Slim plastic boxes for carrying flies and lures.

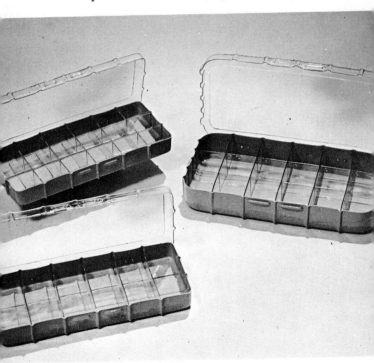

Hook Hone

Dull hooks cost fishermen untold numbers of missed strikes. Fishermen tend to neglect hook points, which should always be kept needle sharp—so sharp that a hook point sticks to your skin if you barely touch it. It is easy to carry a little hook hone and touch up your hook point frequently. It will certainly up your fishing score if you will do it.

Landing Nets

Landing nets vary, of course, depending on whether they are to be carried on your person or in a boat. As a general rule, a boat net should be generously big, a carried net rather small. In fact, folding nets have become increasingly popular with wading fishermen.

Standard landing net for wading.

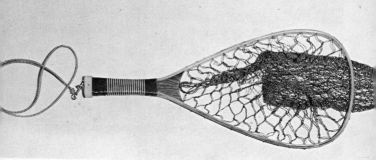

Collapsible landing net in folded position . . .

. . . springs open for instant use.

Creels

Some men still prefer the big basket creel, but there are now canvas creels which work on the old desert-waterbag principle of cooling by evaporation.

The canvas bag is soaked in the water (a plastic flap keeps the wearer dry). Slow, continuous evaporation then keeps the creel's contents cool. These canvas creels are available with a shoulder strap or can be clipped onto the fishing vest.

The boat fisherman uses a stringer rather than a creel, and doesn't need a fishing vest when he can carry along a tackle satchel.

Canvas creel designed like a desert water bag keeps fish cool by evaporation.

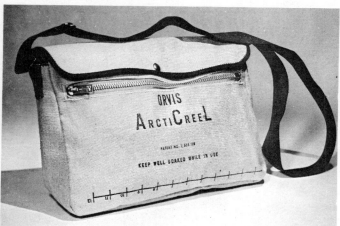

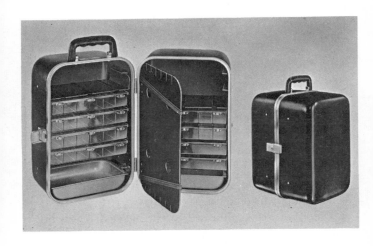

Modern tackle satchels are roomy and efficient. Made of plastic, they are rustproof and quiet in a boat.

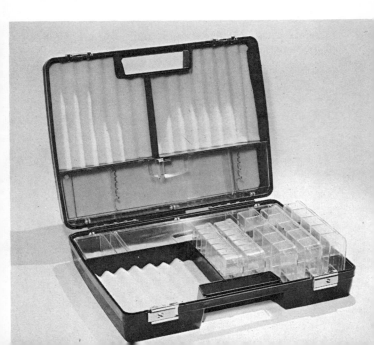

Tackle Satchels

Tackle satchels have come a long way from the relatively clumsy models of just a few years ago. These differences in design are real functional improvements. The fact that they are now largely made of plastic is, alone, an improvement of major importance. Plastic doesn't rust. Plastic is much less noisy in your boat. And well-organized storage space is *important* to the fisherman. A man catches no fish when his lure is not in the water. Fumbling through a tangled mess of tackle can waste a lot of time.

Hooks

Most fishermen, as has been often remarked in these pages, tend to use equipment that is larger and heavier than is wise or necessary for the fishing to be done. Any experienced fly fisherman knows that a 4-pound brown trout can be successfully handled on midge flies tied on tiny #18 or #20 hooks. Hook sizes run in reverse, that is, a #18 is much much smaller than a #6. A #6 is a *large* hook for most freshwater fishing, even for lunker bass. Some bass bugs are made with #4s, #2s, even #1/0s but this is to assure enough gap between lure body and hook point.

Actually, for most bait fishing a #6 hook is large enough. Obviously the smaller a hook the more surely your strike will sink the hook point in past the barb and so prevent the fish's throwing the bait or lure. Also, many warmwater spe-

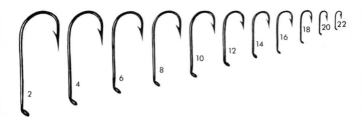

Actual sizes of fishhooks most used in freshwater angling.

cies have small mouths. Even the big-mouthed ones may be in a mood to nibble rather than gulp. So within reason, the smaller your hooks the fewer strikes you miss. The only disadvantage to bait hooks much smaller than #6 is the difficulty of removing the hook from a fish you wish to release unharmed.

Snelled hooks (with heavy monofilament permanently attached) are pretty much out of fashion. Fishermen, whether using flies, lures, or baits, wisely prefer to buy simple eyed hooks and use a single-strand monofilament leader between the line point and the hook. Flyrodders may use tapered leaders of 7½, 9, 12 feet, or longer, while for lure and bait fishing a level leader from 18 inches up may be sufficient to provide the least visible, most flexible connection between a woven line and hook or lure. Of course the spin fisherman, using the lightest monofilament he dares trust, needs no leader at all and simply knots his mono line directly into the hook eye.

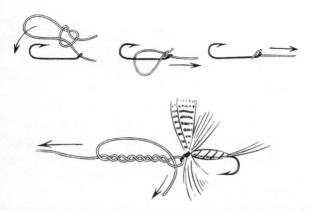

Turle knot (*top*) and clinch knot are both used for tying hook or fly to leader. Turle knot doesn't work well with dry flies; the hackle catches in the loop.

Sinkers

As has been stated before in this book, sinkers are an evil. Sometimes a *necessary* evil, but always to be used as rarely and as sparingly as circumstances permit. One or two split shot may have to be pinched on to carry a lively minnow down to where fish are feeding, or to tumble a worm along the bottom of a fast-moving stream. If the stream is very fast, even more lead may be necessary, in which case it will be found that a pyramid-shaped or tear-drop sinker with a ring top is less inclined to snag than is the old-fashioned cigar-shaped sinker.

14

BOATS AND MOTORS

This discussion of boats will be limited to small craft appropriate for use as fishing platforms on small sheltered waters, and the remarks on motors are limited to those used for slow trolling rather than fast cruising.

The fisherman who has no flotation is a man severely handicapped. Even the wading flyrodder, working streams for trout and smallmouth bass, can sometimes approach difficult (and hence less hard-fished) waters only by floating some sections. The man fishing for bass, panfish, and trout in lakes and ponds simply cannot reach all the productive water by casting from shore.

Boats

From rigged inner tubes, through little backpackable inflatables, on up to big life rafts for shooting white water, the craft that fold small and blow up to wonderfully stable fishing platforms are well worth consideration. The big whitewater boats are designed for special use, of course, and are mentioned here only to call attention to the ruggedness and floatability of inflatables. Their real virtue is their portability.

Harness and zippered seat-and-case for inner tube allows wading fisherman to probe deep-water spots.

For backpacking or flying in to remote water they are the most boat for the least size and weight. They are not very comfortable to sit in and they don't age well, but they are safe, stable flotation which you can take anywhere.

Inflatable boat is a safe fishing platform to pack into remote waters.

A canoe, of aluminum or plastic, is fine sport to paddle, reasonably light to portage, and the traditional craft for wilderness trips. It is not, however, a good fishing platform.

Unless you want an inflatable to carry in to remote beaver ponds, or a canoe to take on a memorable trip down the Allagash, your choice of a fishing boat will probably be in the class known as cartoppers. A cartopper is a boat too bulky and too heavy for long portages over rough terrain but small enough and light enough to carry comfortably on the roof of the family car.

Such a boat should weigh less than 100 pounds, quite a bit less if one man is going to toss it onto a car top. But plenty of such craft do weigh less than 100, and still are roomy enough for one or two fishermen to cast from comfortably.

Some of these are pretty fancy plastic jobs, with all sorts of fittings. Some are aluminum

Typical cartop boat should weigh less than 100 pounds. Even a boat of this size will hold two fishermen with ample casting room.

and plain as a tin can. The boat is in all probability worth the money asked and will make a fine practical fishing craft if it is at least 8 feet long, has at least a 40-inch beam, and weighs no more than you would undertake to load alone in a pinch.

The flat-bottomed, square-ended johnboat is mighty stable and comfortable for sheltered waters. The slightly more seaworthy designs with more freeboard are still not suitable for big water during a heavy windstorm. In fact, no boat a man can load alone is big enough for really rough water.

If you want a big boat you will be limited to using it only when you are fishing with a companion or keeping it moored at a specific location. It is possible for one man alone to load a boat onto a trailer. Nonetheless, any craft other than a small inflatable, a light canoe, or an 80-pound cartopper is really for boating rather than fishing.

Motors

Big motors for fast long-distance travel are not suitable for most types of fishing. Motors for fishing are the light 3 hp (or less) jobs that a man alone can comfortably tote from his car to the water, can mount without risking a hernia, and that move a craft along at slow trolling speed.

Actually, the motors most fairly classified as "fishing accessories" are the electric trolling types, and these are really superb for certain kinds of fishing.

If a man is fishing from a boat alone, and not actually stillfishing from an anchored position, he may spend the better part of his time just maneuvering his craft with oars or paddle. The slightest breeze can become an exasperation. And no matter how carefully he manipulates his oars, some telltale rattle or bump or sweeping motion can spook a lunker bass.

An electric trolling motor can be rigged to be operated by your feet, leaving both hands

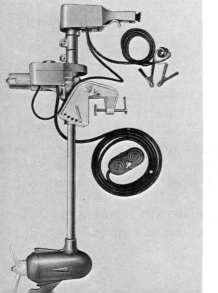

Electric trolling motor can be operated entirely by foot controls, leaving the hand free for casting. Regular car battery supplies power.

free. With a little practice (and it's great fun) you can move your boat, hold it, turn it, snake it into tight spots—all with your feet—while you cast, retrieve, and play your fish with both hands. The gentle hum of the electric motor will not spook fish. The battery for an electric motor is too heavy to portage on a wilderness canoe trip, but for lakes, ponds, and quiet rivers to which a cartop boat can be easily transported, an electric trolling motor is mighty nice.

Fishing in a boat with a companion who will take his turn at the oars is a heartwarming experience. But if boat fishing, especially a lot of trolling, is what you do regularly, a small motor is worth its cost. If it's small enough so that it's not a chore to tote alone, you'll find you really do use it.

INDEX